Department of Education and Science

The Curriculum from 5 to 16

Curriculum Matters 2
AN HMI SERIES

LONDON · HER MAJESTY'S STATIONERY OFFICE

© Crown copyright 1985
First published 1985
ISBN 0 11 270568 5

Contents

	Page
Foreword	1
Introduction	3
The demands on schools	6
Nature and scope of the curriculum	7
Designing the curriculum	13
Assessment	51
Conclusion	54
References	55

# Foreword

This paper is one in a series of discussion documents published by HM Inspectorate under the general title *Curriculum matters*. Over the years the Inspectorate has had much to say about the school curriculum. The need for a series in which this is brought together arose from the announcement by the Secretary of State in his speech in Sheffield in January, 1984, that he intended to seek broad agreement about the objectives of the 5 to 16 curriculum.

The paper seeks to stimulate the professional discussion about the whole curriculum, about the possible basis for agreement, about the broad purposes of primary and secondary education in England and Wales and about the ways in which teachers working in schools might give them expression.

It covers the years 5 to 16 because these are the years of compulsory education and because to treat this span as a whole recognises the need to ensure coherence and progression as pupils move through the system. It also recognises that, although primary and secondary schools differ from one another, both have essentially the same, important educational purposes.

The views expressed in this paper arise from the findings of inspection of existing practice in schools. The HMI survey reports[1,2,3,4] on first, primary, middle and secondary schools and the documents published in connection with the 11 to 16 exercise[5,6,7] carried out jointly within five local education authorities by teachers, advisers and HMI are based on the principle that pupils should have access to a broad, balanced, relevant and coherent curriculum irrespective of the schools they attend. This is because all have in common a need to develop the knowledge, concepts, skills and attitudes necessary for their own development and for playing a full part in modern society.

It is natural that, given its unique heritage, the Welsh language and culture should occupy a distinctive place in the curriculum of schools in Wales. In some, because the Welsh language is in daily use at home and in the community alongside English, it will be accorded a priority in curricular terms similar to that of English. But all children in Welsh schools should have access to the means of extending their familiarity with it and refining it as a means of communication. In addition, the importance of the local context as a starting point for acquiring skills and knowledge, and the intrinsic value of the cultural heritage of Wales, argue for the placing of an appropriate emphasis on a Welsh dimension in the curriculum.

It is hoped that the perceptions and experience reflected in the publications mentioned above give some confidence that the views expressed in this paper represent what might reasonably be expected of schools. It is a discussion document and comments and suggestions from individual readers and from interested associations and institutions will be welcomed. They should be sent by 31 July 1985 to:

Staff Inspector (Curriculum),
Department of Education and Science,
Elizabeth House,
York Road,
London
SE1 7PH

Introduction

1. *Education in schools* (DES and Welsh Office) 1977, *A framework for the school curriculum* (1980) and *The school curriculum* (HMSO, 1981) proposed a number of educational aims for primary and secondary schools. They were:

- to help pupils to develop lively, enquiring minds, the ability to question and argue rationally and to apply themselves to tasks, and physical skills;
- to help pupils to acquire knowledge and skills relevant to adult life and employment in a fast changing world;
- to help pupils to use language and number effectively;
- to instil respect for religious and moral values, and tolerance of other races, religions and ways of life;
- to help pupils to understand the world in which they live, and the interdependence of individuals, groups and nations;
- to help pupils to appreciate human achievements and aspirations.

2. In general these aims command widespread support and they are reflected in the aims drawn up by many local education authorities (LEAs) and individual schools. They apply throughout the years of schooling, to all types of school and across the whole range of ability. Whatever means a school uses to translate its aims into everyday curricular terms, and whatever means it uses to provide appropriately for pupils of different ages and abilities, broad aims of this sort should underlie its day-to-day work in respect of all its pupils.

3. Because schools are an important influence on children's development, both pupils and their parents have a right to expect that education will play its part in helping them to grow up to become competent, confident, rational and self-reliant adults who can manage their own lives and play their part in society. They also have a right to expect that what is taught is what pupils need to know; that it increases their grasp of the subject matter; that it equips them for their future lives and careers; and contributes to a better understanding of themselves and the world in which they live. Individual schools should be able to describe their curricular framework and the means by which they plan to honour their commitment to it. Within that, all pupils should have access to a curriculum of

similar breadth and balance irrespective of their level of ability, the school they attend or their social circumstances. That curriculum appears to be best assured within a coherent framework whose general principles hold good for all schools.

4. The eleven years of compulsory schooling start in infancy and end on the threshold of adulthood. Differences of approach, subject matter, levels of abstraction and complexity to accord with the individual's physical, emotional, social and intellectual development are necessary, but they should not result in a sequence of disparate and unrelated experiences. Much ground can be lost by a failure to build upon the capacities children have already acquired or to recognise in which direction the next step needs to be. Infant, junior, middle and secondary schools of various types have each evolved a range of characteristic organisational and teaching strategies which give each stage its distinctive flavour. This distinctiveness is not at issue. However, it has often been at the root of a disregard of how pupils progress through the system as a whole and of how work at one stage of education and in one kind of school may be made to fit in with that in another. This disregard is most apparent between primary or middle and secondary schools, although it can and does exist between infant and junior departments of the same primary school; between first and middle schools; and between consecutive year groups in the secondary school, particularly years 3 and 4. It brings with it risks of unprofitable repetition and narrow teaching because, in the absence of a well informed appreciation of what has gone before, the tendency is to assume that children have learnt little. If, as a result, the teaching reverts to an undemanding level for the pupils, disillusionment and boredom can set in.

5. To deal adequately with pupils within one phase of education requires a thorough understanding of the educational needs of children in that age range and a view of how a particular phase relates to the whole process. Local Education Authorities have been at pains in recent years to develop policies for the curriculum in their schools which have regard to this unity, as their responses to the Secretary of State's enquiry (*The school curriculum*: Circular 8/83, DES 1983) demonstrate. All schools share a responsibility to promote common aims, so that, although an infant school will differ in many respects from a secondary school, the work of each should promote purposeful teaching and learning that develop lively and enquiring minds, give the enjoyment and satisfaction of doing tasks well, offer challenge appropriate to age and aptitude, and encourage the use of the imagination and powers of reasoning.

6. The Warnock Report[8] described the goals of education as follows:

> They are, first, to enlarge a child's knowledge, experience and imaginative understanding and thus his awareness of moral values and capacity for enjoyment; and secondly, to enable him to enter the world after formal education is over as an active participant in society and a responsible contributor to it, capable of achieving as much independence as possible.

It went on:

> Whereas for some (children) the road they have to travel towards the goals is smooth and easy, for others it is fraught with obstacles. For some the obstacles are so daunting that, even with the greatest possible help, they will not get very far. Nevertheless, for them too, progress will be possible and their educational needs will be fulfilled as they gradually overcome one obstacle after another on the way.

Thus the goals apply to all pupils and to all types of school though in relation to children in special education the extent to which all the goals will be achieved will vary according to whether the pupils require a largely mainstream curriculum with special support, a modified curriculum having objectives more appropriate to their needs, or a developmental curriculum with sharply focused objectives designed to encourage a measure of personal autonomy. For that reason this paper applies to schools in general and does not single out special needs. Its task is to address central professional issues relating to the ways children and young people may be helped to get as far along the road as they can by their own efforts and with the support of others.

7. There is therefore a need for unity of purpose throughout the 5 to 16 age span. That unity needs also to apply across the school system as a whole if the desired range and quality of experience and learning are to have a more assured place than they do now across the country, in LEAs, in individual schools and, above all, in what is offered to individual pupils. The reasons for the diversity of what is offered are themselves various and stem from responses to change, for example in the organisation of schooling, and to a variety of curriculum development projects in different areas of the curriculum. These responses have often been vigorous and have shown a healthy concern for local need and individual opportunity. There have been many examples of real benefits for pupils and teachers from changes in classroom practice. But the response has often been piecemeal, or too concerned with organisational change alone, so that coherent debate and action about the

curriculum as a whole, and about the place of individual components within it, have received less attention. The wide diversity of sizes and types of primary, middle and secondary schools, and the diversity of expectations from school to school and among teachers point to the need for greater consistency in what is offered to, and what might be expected of, pupils of similar potential wherever they may live.

The demands on schools

8. In formulating the aims and objectives on which the curriculum should be built, schools will necessarily have to take account of the policy decisions of LEAs and central government and of the expectations of parents, employers and the community at large. They are properly expected to give attention to academic progress, though not to the exclusion of other important experiences. In delivering a curriculum intended to provide a similar range of learning for all pupils, schools and teachers have to take account of individual differences and aspirations by adapting content and methods to match individual strengths and weaknesses.

9. Schools also have to respond to social changes such as the increased cultural diversity of society, to the impact of technology and to changing patterns of employment. These and other influences are expected to be reflected in the curriculum and they make demands upon the skills of teachers and the limited amount of time available. In meeting these demands, schools are seldom given advice about what might be discarded. Nor is society itself always agreed about how schools should order their priorities. Society looks to schools to solve many of its current problems but, if schools respond to what are often sensitive issues, they are as likely to be criticised by some for dealing with the issues at all, as they are by others for not doing enough.

10. Thus schools have to take account of the varying concerns of all who 'use' the system, in ways which outlive the exigencies of the moment. They are more likely to discharge their responsibilities wisely when they ensure that parents and others understand their intentions and the reasons for them. That is best done on the basis of a clear view of what education is intended to do for all the pupils and to enable them to do for

themselves; what range of knowledge and skills should be included; and what understanding and qualities pupils are to be helped to develop, or to acquire.

Nature and scope of the curriculum

11. A school's curriculum consists of all those activities designed or encouraged within its organisational framework to promote the intellectual personal, social and physical development of its pupils. It includes not only the formal programme of lessons, but also the 'informal' programme of so-called extracurricular activities as well as all those features which produce the school's 'ethos', such as the quality of relationships, the concern for equality of opportunity, the values exemplified in the way the school sets about its task and the way in which it is organised and managed. Teaching and learning styles strongly influence the curriculum and in practice they cannot be separated from it. Since pupils learn from all these things, it needs to be ensured that all are consistent in supporting the school's intentions.

12. The curriculum should aim to be broad by bringing all pupils into contact with an agreed range of areas of learning and experience. It should also be balanced in that it allows the adequate development of each area. In addition, each major component should have breadth, balance and relevance and should incorporate a progression in the acquisition of knowledge and understanding. The various curricular areas should reinforce and complement one another so that the knowledge, concepts, skills and attitudes developed in one area may be put to use and provide insight in another, thus increasing the pupils' understanding, competence and confidence.

13. Certain organisational features of primary, secondary and special schools facilitate the provision of a curriculum which meets these requirements while others tend to inhibit it. The class teacher system in primary schools has the advantage of giving the younger children sustained contact with one teacher who will know the overall pattern of their work and so be able to identify their needs over the whole curriculum. The main disadvantage of this system is that few individual teachers can be so expert in every part of the curriculum as to ensure that the special features of each subject or area make their full contribution to the education of the older children. Secondary schools,

which have the expertise in subjects, often find that their form of organisation – in departments or faculties, for example – makes it difficult to interrelate different parts of the curriculum and for any one teacher to see the needs of the pupil as a whole. Because special schools are relatively small and sometimes serve a wide age range, they tend to reflect some of the organisational features of both primary and secondary schools and may experience some of the limitations and strengths of each. In all types of school, identifying the range of knowledge, concepts, skills, and attitudes to be gained through the work in hand and teaching accordingly help to ensure that each activity makes as full a contribution as possible.

14. Within the curriculum as a whole, teachers are concerned also with the personal development of individual pupils, with their welfare and with helping them to gain satisfaction and maximum benefit from their experiences in school. In primary schools responsibility for pastoral care, guidance and counselling generally rests with class teachers, who know the children well and who carry out these tasks informally with support from the head. Secondary schools usually include timetabled tutorial periods but opportunities for pupils to reflect on their experiences and express their individual needs arise in the course of work in all parts of the curriculum. All teachers thus have a part to play in caring, guiding and advising, whether on personal, educational or vocational matters.

The teaching programme

15. In primary schools the teaching programme may be planned in a variety of ways. Parts of the programme for the younger children may be organised through carefully planned activities, such as domestic role play and the use of constructional toys, within which desired knowledge and understanding can be developed through skilful intervention by the teacher and the provision of selected resources for learning. For older primary pupils it may take the form of themes or topics closely linked to the children's interests and experiences, or of separate subjects, or of some combination of these. For example, the term environmental studies may be used to cover various elements of subjects in combination, such as geography and history together with science, language, art, craft and possibly drama. Important aspects such as health education may be treated separately, or may permeate a number of subject areas.

16. It is for individual schools to decide how the curriculum is to be organised for teaching purposes, but each of these ways of organising the work in primary schools has to be assessed in terms of its fitness for purpose. Topic work, for example, has potential advantages in facilitating sustained work on themes which children find interesting and relevant; in providing blocks of time suitable for educational visits and practical activities; and in giving opportunities for the development of knowledge, concepts, study and other skills and attitudes associated with several areas of learning. It can be economical of time in that a single experience, such as a visit to a farm, can give rise to work in several areas of learning each of which would require a fresh stimulus if pursued separately. Yet it can be difficult to ensure that there is sufficient progression and continuity, particularly for older children, in the work in each area covered by a topic and it may be easier to plan progression if some of the work is organised as separate subjects.

17. In secondary schools subjects are well established as a convenient and familiar way of organising learning, and in their selection of subjects they try to ensure for their pupils a broad, balanced and useful education. It is to be expected that secondary schools will wish to begin at this point, since one of their strengths lies in subjects well taught by staff with specialised training and experience. Outside the schools, the notion of subjects is familiar to parents and the public at large, and certain aspects of subjects relate directly to both general and specific requirements of employment or social life.

18. However, there are limitations in a curriculum which is no more than a list of subjects. For example, it is too easy to define the content of each subject with no reference whatever to the learning processes to be used or to what is happening in the rest of the curriculum, especially in the later years of secondary education where the real and perceived needs of examinations are very influential. This may lead to a situation in which, although pupils may be following courses in a number of subjects, the range of activities they are required to undertake is small and the curriculum which they actually experience is narrow. The national secondary survey[4] recorded curricula in many schools, which, especially in years 4 and 5, were heavily dominated by writing, largely of a kind requiring notes and summaries. In consequence talk tended to be squeezed out, especially that type of talk which helps young people to handle new ideas, to develop a reasoned argument, to internalise their

experiences and to find personal expression for them. To teach each subject without close reference to others, or to an overall framework of educational objectives, is to risk losing that very breadth and 'wholeness' which most schools, in their aims, undertake to provide. Important skills, for example the ability to draw upon information from a variety of sources to help solve a problem, may be substantially neglected; and the opportunity for knowledge and insight gained in one subject to be reinforced in another may not be taken. Where the curriculum is defined only in subjects, it is difficult to accommodate those aspects which tend to fall between the subject boundaries; for example, environmental education, economic awareness, and social education and new needs such as computer education. Curricular development may become nothing more than a matter of negotiating room on the timetable for extras intended for some pupils, rather than one of improving the whole curricular diet for all, and teaching it more effectively.

Learning and teaching approaches

19. The influence of learning activities and teaching styles on what is learned and how well it is learned has already been noted. The more the curriculum includes objectives which go beyond subject matter and promote the development of particular attitudes and capabilities, the stronger are the implications for the variety and range of teaching approaches to be employed if all the objectives are to be achieved. As far as possible, teaching should match the abilities, attainments, interests and experience of pupils; in addition to factual knowledge, it is important to develop concepts, skills and attitudes, and pupils should learn in a variety of ways according to the task in hand. It follows that no single style of teaching will be suitable for all purposes; sometimes it will be appropriate to teach the class as a whole; sometimes pupils should carry considerable responsibility for deciding the direction of their work. To achieve some objectives, for example mastering the skills of analysis and constructing a reasoned argument, it will be necessary for pupils to talk through a problem, to try out hypotheses, or conduct a practical experiment; and in all cases it will be important for teachers to assess how far pupils are succeeding and how they need to be helped. The assessment should include performance related to the various learning objectives across the whole range of activities.

20. The curriculum in this broad sense provides a context for learning which, as well as providing for the progressive

development of knowledge, understanding and skills, recognises and builds on the particular developmental characteristics of childhood and adolescence. Active learning, and a sense of purpose and success, enhance pupils' enjoyment, interest, confidence and sense of personal worth; passive learning and inappropriate teaching styles can lead to frustration and failure. In particular, it is necessary to ensure that the pupils are given sufficient first-hand experience, accompanied by discussion, upon which to base abstract ideas and generalisations. Teaching and learning might, for example, extend to using the local environment, undertaking community service and establishing contact with commerce and industry. The national primary survey[2] found that the work children were given to do was better matched to their abilities when teachers employed a combination of didactic and exploratory approaches. The national secondary survey[4] pointed to the care needed to avoid teaching styles developing within subjects and across the curriculum as a whole which overemphasise the abstract and the theoretical at the expense of the experimental and the practical; writing at the expense of talking; factual knowledge at the expense of skills and understanding; and narrowly prescribed work at the expense of that in which pupils might use their own initiative.

Pupil grouping

21. Many forms of grouping, from individual teaching to a whole-school assembly, have a part to play through the variety of experiences which they can provide, as well as the opportunities which they offer to match learning tasks to the characteristics of the pupils. Schools, departments and individual teachers need to keep this in mind when selecting the form of organisation which is to be employed for a particular piece of work.

22. In primary schools, and many special schools, children are arranged in groups of various sizes and for a variety of purposes. A class session may be an economical way of giving instruction, introducing thematic work, or practising certain kinds of oral work; individual teaching may be required in the early stages of reading; and pupils benefit, for example, from practising particular oral, mathematical and physical skills in small groups of two or three. Different groupings can influence what is learned as well as how it is learned. Task groups where the children are asked to work together, for example, to devise a

sequence of movements, or to compose a musical accompaniment, can encourage children to cooperate, to share ideas, to listen to one another and to appreciate the contributions made by other people. Interest groups can give children opportunities to share enthusiasms, to extend present interests and develop new ones. Grouping according to ability, attainment and experience is one means by which teachers provide differentiated work to cater for differences among the children. Group work makes a positive contribution to the children's learning because it recognises similarities among them as well as differences and enables the children to learn from and interact with one another. Furthermore the teacher is able to give more sustained attention to a group than could be given to each individual within it.

23. For secondary schools and for older pupils in special schools the principles are similar but the tasks and the opportunities are different. As pupils grow older their interests and aptitudes become more sharply focused and developed. A greater differentiation of treatment is called for which, with the greater degree of subject specialisation, results in a complex organisational structure. The presence of a larger number of teachers in secondary schools offers the greater possibility of grouping for different purposes: for example, subject sets or remedial groups can be formed to enable pupils of broadly similar aptitudes to work together. Organisational arrangements can be made which enable several teachers to be deployed at one time so that, for example, team and cooperative teaching may be employed; the size of groups and the range of ability in them can also be varied according to the learning in hand.

24. General organisational arrangements within the school do not absolve teachers and departments from using a variety of arrangements within their classes to suit different purposes. Flexibility is necessaary if the various types of grouping are to match the learning which it is planned should take place: instruction may be to the whole class; explanation and application may involve small groups or individuals; discussion may occupy small groups; experimental and practical work, as in science or CDT, may be based on groups of two or three pupils. The improvements in pupil : teacher ratios that have taken place in recent years make it possible for many schools to adopt more flexible arrangements, but in the main they have been used to bring about small overall reductions in class size.

Designing the curriculum

25. In this paper the overall curricular framework is viewed from two essential and complementary perspectives: first, **areas of learning and experience** (*paragraph 32*) and second, **elements of learning,** that is, the knowledge, concepts, skills and attitudes to be developed (*paragraph 90*). These perspectives are not in conflict with the ways in which schools commonly organise teaching and learning; topics, themes or subjects need to support some or all of the facets of the 'whole education' which the two perspectives describe in helping to achieve the school's aims and objectives.

26. There are some essential issues which are not necessarily contained within subjects, but which need to be included in the curriculum. While they may sometimes be taught separately they are more frequently and often more appropriately mediated through topics, subjects, groups of subjects or the general life of the school. Some of these issues are listed in the following paragraphs. Whatever the arrangements for cross-curricular issues, they should not be left to chance or to individual initiatives; their place needs to be assured through consultation, be consistent with the general framework adopted by the school, and be recorded in schemes of work which indicate the progression to be expected.

27. **Environmental education,** which can help pupils to develop an awareness, appreciation and understanding of their surroundings, may be presented through science, history and geography, for example, or can act as a unifying approach for work in and out of school in several subjects and curricular areas. **Health education,** essential for pupils' physical and moral well-being, may be promoted through the medium of topic work, subjects of the curriculum or special courses. **Information technology,** which is having a profound effect on pupils whose adult lives will be in the 21st century, should find a place in all subjects which are able to take advantage of the facility to store and process information and to generate further information. **Political education,** important if pupils are to understand the forces, issues and processes at work in society, may be dealt with, not only through such subjects such as history, geography and social studies, but also through science, CDT, business studies and literature as well as through aspects of school life which exemplify the workings of society at large. **Education in economic understanding** is also important in helping pupils to come to understand the economic system and

the general factors which influence it, some of them contentious. At secondary level business studies and other subjects such as mathematics, CDT, history and geography can contribute to the development of economic understanding; pupils can be actively involved at an individual level through their own personal budgetting and collectively in schools through such activities as running a school bookshop, mini-companies and school societies.

28. A sound general education should **prepare young people for the world of work.** In doing so schools have to build on the pupil's experience and perceptions gained from everyday life outside the school – in families, in shops and often (in respect of older pupils) in Saturday and holiday jobs. But schools have the responsibility to develop in their pupils, progressively throughout the primary and secondary years, the understanding, skills and attitudes which enhance their opportunities and provide a sound basis of competence and commitment for their future lives and work. Essentially these are that pupils should be articulate, literate and numerate. They should have some understanding of people and what prompts them to think and act as they do, and be able to interact and work with others as well as to operate independently. Their experiences in school should foster enjoyment in learning, a sense of curiosity, pride in their work, a concern for quality and accuracy, personal initiative and integrity and the determination to persevere at a task. Pupils should also encounter problem-solving design processes and become familiar with new technology. In addition, they should be well informed about the world in which they live; the human, political, economic, social and environmental factors that influence and shape it; and how and why it came to be as it is. Within this broad picture pupils should develop some understanding of the place of industry, trade, commerce and public services in the scheme of things and be aware of the factors that influence them.

29. **Careers education** needs to be timetabled in the later years of secondary education and to involve cooperation with the careers service. Often it is concentrated in years four and five, following preparation in year three for option choices; but perceptions of self and work begin to develop in early childhood. Young people need to broaden their horizons so that they do not unthinkingly fall in with traditional attitudes. Girls especially need to be encouraged to keep options open by continuing with a spread of subjects, including the physical sciences and technology, while boys need encouragement to

continue with foreign languages. Careers education involves learning about oneself and about opportunities post-16 and using this awareness to make informed decisions. Many parts of the curriculum can contribute to this process and it is necessary to coordinate these contributions. In a world in which a pupil's future may include several changes of occupation and periods of unemployment, it is the more important that careers education should be concerned with personal development and should set employment in the general context of adult life. The partnership of the school, parents and the wider community is crucial.

30. Schools on their own cannot combat the influences which dispose boys and girls readily to accept or to seek for themselves conventional sex-linked roles. Outside schools, and especially within families, such sex-stereotyping is commonly reinforced: often the measures schools take to reduce it are not supported by parents. Nevertheless, schools have a responsibility to promote **equal opportunities for girls and boys,** and to ensure that this policy is supported in the way in which those opportunities are presented, in staff attitudes, and in the organisation and day to day running of the school.

31. Schools which have pupils from **ethnic minority groups** should ensure that the curriculum, in addition to meeting any specific language learning needs they may have, offers them stimulus and opportunity for success. They should be helped to enter fully into a British society which recognises, respects and draws upon their own culture and traditions within a context which emphasises that which is common to and shared by all. The curriculum in those schools which have no pupils from ethnic minority groups should similarly be of a kind which opens the minds of the pupils to other traditions and other ways of viewing the world, and which challenges and dispels the ignorance and distrust which breed racial prejudice and discrimination.

Areas of learning and experience

32. The areas of learning and experience listed and described below embody a point of view about the broad lines of development which should feature in a rounded education. No claim is made that this is the only possible, or an original, point of view. It provides only one perspective: another, which complements it, concerns knowledge, concepts, skills and attitudes and is considered in *paragraphs 90 to 105*.

Areas of learning and experience—continued

33. The curriculum of all schools should involve pupils in each of the following areas of learning and experience:

aesthetic and creative

human and social

linguistic and literary

mathematical

moral

physical

scientific

spiritual

technological.

These are not suggested as discrete elements to be taught separately and in isolation from one another. They constitute a planning and analytical tool. Nor are they equated with particular subjects (for example, pupils may gain scientific or mathematical experience from art, and aesthetic experience from mathematics), although inevitably individual subjects contribute more to some areas than to others. Issue such as environmental education and preparation for the world of work are a feature of all or several of the areas, although the emphasis and nature of such work will differ from area to area.

34. Schools should ensure that, however the work of pupils is organised, each of the above areas of learning and experience is represented sufficiently for it to make its unique contribution, part of which is to assist in the development of knowledge, concepts, skills and attitudes which can be learnt, practised and applied in many parts of the curriculum. For example, scientific learning introduces the practical experiment as a means of investigating observed phenomena, while offering valuable opportunities to develop more general skills such as approaching tasks in a logical manner, communicating information and ideas, and observing and recording. A single activity can contribute to several areas of learning. When learning to cook, for example, six year olds can extend their vocabulary and oral skills; learn to recognise simple mathematical relationships; be trained in hygiene; and improve their manual dexterity.

35. Schools need to examine existing practice to establish the extent to which particular topics, aspects and subjects are already contributing to these areas and to the development of

knowledge, concepts, skills and attitudes. They will then be in a position to decide on any changes and additions which may be required. The following section provides descriptions of the nine areas of learning and experience, not as definitive statements, but as a basis for further discussion in schools.

Aesthetic and creative

36. This area is concerned with the capacity to respond emotionally and intellectually to sensory experience; the awareness of degrees of quality; and the appreciation of beauty and fitness for purpose. It involves the exploration and understanding of feeling and the processes of making, composing and inventing. Aesthetic and creative experience may occur in any part of the curriculum, but some subjects contribute particularly to the development of pupils' aesthetic awareness and understanding because they call for personal, imaginative, affective and often practical, responses to sensory experience. Art, crafts, design, some aspects of technology, music, dance, drama and theatre arts, in particular, promote the development of the imagination and the creative use of media and materials.

37. There are two interrelated strands in the development of aesthetic awareness and understanding in schools. One manifests itself through pupils creating their own works, whether pictures, models, music, plays, mimes or poems; the other comes from experiencing, interpreting or performing the works of other people such as artists, composers, writers or architects. These two strands are mutually enriching and pupils need to interpret what they have heard, seen and felt at the same time as they try to express their own understandings and feelings in suitable media. They require sources of inspiration and they need to acquire a range of resources and techniques which is gradually extended as pictures are painted, music is composed and played, or plays are devised and acted.

38. Through drawing, painting, modelling, carving, designing and constructing, pupils should acquire knowledge and skills and develop perceptions which enable them to make a personal response to what they see, touch and feel. Primary age children can begin to consider the importance of the choice of medium in creating a particular effect, while older pupils may examine the relationship between aesthetics and fitness for purpose in design. The exploration of sound should help pupils to discover ways in which chosen sounds can be sequenced and combined to form musical compositions, and to appreciate that

Areas of learning and experience—continued

in ways peculiar to it music may both express and generate ideas and feelings. Their enjoyment of music may be enhanced through hearing live performances, learning how best to use their voices and through developing the necessary intrumental techniques to devise their own pieces. The use of the human body as a means of communicating ideas and feelings and interpreting the meanings of others is most clearly seen in the various forms of dance and drama. Dance may range from the creation, by the children, of their own dance sequences to convey meaning and feeling to a highly structured country dance where the pattern of movement is strictly determined and must match the rhythm and pattern of the music precisely. Experience in drama sometimes takes the form of visits to theatres, or participation in performances or workshops in school. Young children should have opportunities for imaginative role play and improvised drama while older pupils benefit from opportunities to devise, write, direct, design and perform plays. These experiences can contribute to growth in self-confidence and understanding in aesthetic judgements. In secondary schools the experiences should also extend into film and television where pupils have particular interests and concerns and where they often need to be able to exercise critical judgements.

39. Knowledge and skills thus acquired can make a valuable contribution to other areas of learning and experience. For example, the drawing of plants in science can increase the pupils' understanding and ability to observe; making music of different styles and periods can evoke the spirit of cultures and ages other than our own; and through dance and drama pupils can explore matters of importance to them such as family life and personal relationships.

40. Experience of making, performing, composing and inventing can help pupils to appreciate and to make informed judgements about the works of others, can educate pupils in the uses and characteristics of various media such as paint and sound, and can help to prepare them for work and for leisure.

Human and social

41. This area is concerned with people and how they live, with their relationships with each other and with their environment, and how human action, now and in the past, has

influenced events and conditions. Pupils need to understand that human beings, in shaping their world, making their living, planning their futures, developing forms of government and law, are influenced to a greater or lesser degree by ideas and beliefs, by their past, by the places and conditions in which they live and by the ways in which they need to relate to each other. The choice of themes, topics or subjects through which to approach this work should introduce essential facts and concepts, develop general skills and use pupils' own experiences where possible as starting points. Pupils' families and surroundings are resources on which schools can draw in planning their work, especially in the earlier years, and provide a valuable basis for broader considerations at a later stage. Literature, the classics, foreign languages, drama and art can all be used as sources of information and discussion to enable pupils to develop an understanding of people and events in different historical and cultural contexts, and of people and places in different geographical circumstances.

42. In learning about people and how they live, pupils should be helped to appreciate that the present world grew out of the past. The themes which are studied should allow them to look for similarities and differences; to try to explain how and why change did or did not occur; and to develop a sense of chronological sequence. The important question, 'How do we know about the past?' can lead to opportunities for pupils to use historical evidence in the form of primary source material such as pictures, objects, written records and the memories of people still alive. Knowledge and experience which are provided in the classroom should enable pupils to imagine what it was like to live in another period, to avoid anachronism and to begin to distinguish between fantasy and historical imagination. Choosing the content is a crucial matter since the act of selection and rejection can appear to affirm or deny the importance or significance of given groups of people, or of particular social, political and economic arrangements. The content should also inform young people about the world in which they live and should, therefore, have not only local and British elements but also a world dimension, as well as drawing on a wide variety of historical epochs.

43. Pupils should be helped to explore and investigate the area in which they live, and they should undertake studies which enable them to develop an appreciation and understanding of the variety of physical and human conditions on the

Areas of learning and experience—*continued*

Earth's surface and the ways men and women have come to terms with them and have brought about change. Investigating the processes which produce geographical variety and pattern and which bring about change requires that attention be given to areas which range in spatial scale from the comparatively small and localised, as in the case of an individual farm or a shopping centre, to the regional, national and global. The complex relationships between people and their environment and the significance to people's lives of the location of places and activities, and of the links between places, and of the place of economic, social and political activity, should form persistent themes within such studies. The content which is selected should enable pupils to examine the different ways in which people react to, modify and shape their surroundings; the ways in which changes of location and of spatial relationships are brought about and the effects of these changes; and how environmental conditions influence economic social and political activities. Pupils should be helped to appreciate how improvements in transport and communications tend to strengthen the interdependence of communities and of nations. Opportunities should be given for pupils to enquire into important issues concerned with the quality of the environment and with geographical variations in human welfare. Suitable attention should be given to the use and interpretation of maps, while direct experience and enquiry should, where possible, be provided through work in the field.

44. From an early age, children are aware that there is a 'world of work' in which many of their relatives are engaged. Throughout the 5 to 16 period this awareness should be built upon so that during the secondary stage pupils come to understand the part played by industry, trade and commerce and services in sustaining the economic, social and cultural life of society: that while they are governed by forces such as supply and demand they are in turn sustained and shaped by the quality of human actions.

45. In infant schools, learning about the work of postmen, shopkeepers, nurses, policemen and other people who are seen at work by the children in their everyday lives lays a good foundation. Later studies should help children to appreciate the large number of interdependent jobs within an economy which encompasses a wide range of manufacturing industries, services, public utilities and technologies. Later, pupils ought

to know the broad outlines of the economy of their own country, to see how its workings depend on and contrast with other economies and to understand the basic principles of economics. They should also come to some understanding of the nature and structure of their own society, its culture, institutions and values. British society, in all its variety, must be put into an historical and geographical context so that pupils can see what they do and do not share with people living in other places and nations and at different times. Much of that which forms children's views about the society in which they live comes from sources outside the school: newspapers, television, talking with family and friends. Work dealing with human and social questions should bear this in mind and equip children to be objective and critical in their handling of a wide variety of source materials. In social matters how one learns is as important as what one learns.

Linguistic and literary

46. This area is concerned with increasing pupils' command of language in listening, speaking, reading and writing. In part this will be achieved through the use of language for a variety of purposes in home and school, in part through the specific study of language and literature.

47. In order to work effectively, primary teachers should build on the language experience and skills which children possess on entry to school. It is, perhaps, insufficiently recognised that secondary teachers should begin with a similar understanding of their pupils' varied competences on entry to the secondary phase. All schools should provide a variety of contexts in which pupils may learn to respond to and use language for a variety of purposes. Language is generated and extended through the interaction of listening, speaking, reading, writing and experience. For example, young children who have made models in clay or who have listened to a story which has moved and informed them, are usually eager to talk about the experience. In doing so they clarify and extend both their thinking and their language, which assists them in their writing.

48. Through listening and talking in groups children are enabled to explore other people's experiences and to modify and extend their own. This mutually reinforcing process deepens the understanding of the experience itself and prompts the development of their language. All pupils need to be given ample opportunity for discussion of a wide range of experiences

Areas of learning and experience—continued

encountered inside and outside school. The narration of their diaries by infants to their teacher can give practice in the ordering and sharing of information and feelings. Investigations in science can promote accurate description from direct observation, awareness of similarities and differences and speculation about cause and effect. Such activities provide opportunities for the teacher to sharpen the focus, extend the comment and prompt further speculation. Faced with such challenges children often need, not only to draw on their resources of vocabulary and familiar forms of expression, but also to try out new ways of expressing the meaning they want to convey. It is at this point, when there is a context of shared experience and an urgent need to communicate that the teacher's help can be most effective.

49. A range of language skills and competences needs to be developed throughout the years of schooling and across all subjects. Pupils should learn to speak with confidence, clarity and fluency, using forms of speech appropriate for a variety of audiences, involving a variety of situations and groupings and for a range of purposes of increasing complexity and demand. As they progress through the early stages of reading they should learn to read fluently, and with understanding, a range of different kinds of material, using methods appropriate to the material and the purposes for which they are reading; to have confidence in their capacities as readers; to enjoy reading for entertainment, for interest and for information; and to appreciate the necessity of reading for learning in most areas of the curriculum and for their personal lives. The pupils should write for a range of purposes; organise the content in ways appropriate to the purposes; use styles of writing appropriate to them and to the intended readership; and use spelling, punctuation and syntax accurately and with confidence. Pupils need to achieve a working knowledge of language so that they have a vocabulary for discussing it and are able to use it with greater awareness and control. That which characterises the achievement of older pupils is not only the accumulation of new knowledge or skills, but an increased ability to use language with sensitivity, sophistication and discrimination and to deal with more demanding forms of spoken and written language used by others.

50. Language is used in all areas of the 5 to 16 curriculum; it is the means of clarifying and of communicating the ideas which

define relationships and establish patterns of working. Usually its form and vocabulary are similar in most subjects. Less commonly, it is used in a subject-specific sense where vocabulary carries a different meaning or emphasis from common usage, and where forms may take on a specialised character. Pupils should be encouraged to explore ideas which are new to them in their own words before being introduced to the technical terms for those ideas. Teachers in all subjects need to be proficient users of language themselves and to be aware of the difficulties which pupils may encounter when faced with new concepts expressed in technical vocabulary.

51. Works of literature, including those of other countries and of the ancient world, portray every aspect of human experience and bring that experience into sharp focus by refining both thought and language. The reading of literature, as well as being valuable in its own right, is, therefore, and essential part of the experience of language at all ages: it can extend pupils' understanding and sympathies and has a part to play in developing judgement. It can also illuminate many areas of the curriculum by the vividness and directness with which it can provide new experiences for some pupils and extend the experiences of others. Subjects such as history already use literary sources freely and many others could do so with advantage.

52. Experience of language is extended and linguistic awareness increased by knowledge of a second language. The fact that many children from ethnic minority groups speak two languages, English at school and another language at home, can help to create a context of reality for work in foreign languages. Almost all pupils in secondary schools embark on the study of a foreign language (and/or Welsh as a second language in the schools of Wales), although too many of them abandon their study after two or three years; there is evidence, however, that the provision of more practical goals is helping to encourage greater interest at this stage. At its best foreign language learning achieves ready and accurate understanding, and intelligible and fluent use, of the spoken and written word, though necessarily over a narrower range and with less complexity of language use than in the case of the mother tongue. Foreign language study expands the linguistic area of experience by affording interesting linguistic comparisons. It also offers insight into another culture and as such is concerned with the human and social area of experience; concepts such as number, weight and time can be reinforced in foreign language learning. Throughout the course pupils can be encouraged to

Areas of learning and experience—continued

view the familiar from a different angle, not least in terms of people's behaviour, and thereby widen horizons and break down feelings of insularity.

53. Courses in the classical languages have undergone a radical change of emphasis in recent years. While retaining the aim of a sound grammatical knowledge of the language, modern courses seek above all to encourage fluent, perceptive and critical reading of Greek or Latin literature, set within the context of the world that produced it. Teachers seek to impart the essential linguistic skills, and through these to promote an understanding of the structure of language and its complexities and an awareness of subtlety of expression and shades of meaning; and at the same time to encourage a critical approach to literature and a sensitivity to the similarities and differences between the classical and modern worlds.

Mathematical

54. For some pupils competence in mathematics will become a particularly important acquisition, either in its own right, or because of its application in science, engineering and many other branches of learning. But all pupils need to learn a variety of mathematical concepts and processes if they are to understand and appreciate relationships and pattern in both number and space in their everyday lives and be able to express them clearly and concisely.

55. Mathematics is taught to virtually all pupils for the whole period of compulsory schooling. Many children in primary schools find enjoyment and excitement in mathematical work, whether it occurs within the lessons devoted to the subject, or elsewhere in the curriculum, especially when it is varied and applied to real situations. At best, they learn that mathematical ideas can be talked about and experimented with, and that they can be used along with other ideas to solve a problem, or express a point of view. As pupils proceed through the secondary school, there is too often a tendency for mathematical procedures to be taught at the expense of pupils' involvement and understanding, with the result that many find the subject increasingly difficult and unappealing. It is always important to explore a problem in familiar terms in order to decide upon, and understand the working of, a particular mathematical process.

56. Although mathematics at one level is probably the most abstract of subjects, it should often arise from, and give rise to, extensive practical activity and investigation. The range of mathematical experience to which pupils are exposed ought therefore to be as broad as possible. Young children should be introduced to mathematics through guided play with materials such as sand and water, and through shopping and domestic play. These can give experience in a range of mathematical topics including capacity and money, and provide opportunities for discrimination, classification and quantitative description. As children get older their needs and interests change but there is still a fundamental need, throughout their schooling, for their mathematical development to be grounded in relevant, practical experiences. There is strong evidence to suggest that, where there is this emphasis, mastery of the so-called basic skills is more likely to occur than when there is a narrow concentration on the skills themselves.

57. All pupils need to be encouraged to respond orally and to discuss their work. This will help them to clarify their own thoughts, to tackle real life problems which are drawn from a variety of experiences in and out of school and to carry out mathematical investigations. In addition it will help the teacher to assess their level of understanding. Development of pupils' capacity for reasoning, including logical deduction, should be encouraged, for example, in connection with everyday things and activities encountered in the classroom, at home or out of doors.

58. Mathematical concepts and processes involving, for example, number, order, weight, length, time, money, computation and formulae receive attention in mathematics lessons. The mathematical area is much broader than this, however, and is dealt with not only in the teaching of the subject itself but also in other activities and subjects of the curriculum. It is to be found, for example, in topic work, art, science, home economics, craft and geography, where the mathematical experience may include the construction of geometrical designs, making graphs, costing, estimating and measuring in planning a meal, quantifying results and using grid references. Older pupils should see that in all kinds of speech and writing mathematical concepts are present, sometimes in linguistic forms such as analogy or in considerations of magnitude and spatial relationships. Mathematical experiences are also linked with aesthetic experiences, for example in the consideration of the proportions of a building, or the physical balance of the gymnast.

Areas of learning and experience—*continued*

Moral

59. The school community, like family life, provides a context for moral learning and experience in a number of ways. First, it brings together moral actions and the principles which underlie them. If pupils are to understand concepts such as fairness and justice, they must see those concepts exemplified by the adults with whom they deal. Second, it provides experiences which help to form and test moral convictions and to modify attitudes. It serves as an arena in which pupils can come to terms with the fact that the views and feelings of others must be taken into account; that the interests of the institution must be weighed against those of individuals; and that the rational resolution of disagreement is possible and desirable.

60. In addition to this practical moral learning, however, is the necessity for pupils to begin the process of reasoning about morality. There is a place in schools for some direct moral teaching, but older pupils in particular must be helped to reason about values if they are to make sound moral judgements.

61. Children should be able to feel that their school has a clear, consistent and secure moral framework, which will help them to explore those moral questions which affect them, and which often concern adult society as well. The place of discussion in moral learning from its earliest stages cannot be overemphasised. With both younger and older children it will frequently arise spontaneously from current events and from incidents in school life, or be consciously stimulated by the teacher bringing to notice, for example, the choices that have to be made about a particular course of action. Although morality and religion are not the same thing, religious education is one of the subject areas which can contribute to moral development. But important though it is, it is only one, and much can be and is achieved through other parts of the curriculum. For example, in games pupils gain experience of acting within a code of rules and of patterning relationships both in cooperation and competition according to them. The study of literature and drama provides many opportunities for a consideration of the way characters in a story behave and why. In topic and project work pupils may need to consider the motivation of people in the recent and more distant past, and there, as in science and geography, pupils will begin to meet the questions of social

morality which are involved in such matters as man's responsibility for the environment.

62. Because so much moral education is carried on incidentally in schools, there is a temptation to assume that school life and the normal programme of work will produce a sufficiently broad range of experiences. This is not necessarily so. Schools need to examine what they provide intentionally as well as that which arises incidentally from the programme of work in order to ensure that pupils are given sufficient information and opportunities to use their initiative and to make informed choices; to exercise leadership and responsibility; to consider the consequences of their own actions; and to develop positive moral qualities.

63. In many secondary schools issues of personal and social morality are dealt with in specific courses for older pupils which include elements of religious education, health and social education, and careers education. These courses can be valuable when they have sufficient substance to enable pupils to engage in informed discussion of issues which bear upon the individual and society. However, the whole of the formal curriculum, the informal activities and relationships of the school community and, not least, the example of those in authority, all make powerful contributions. Indeed, all that happens in schools provides occasions for pupils to form attitudes and to draw conclusions about human relationships.

64. For many voluntary schools it will be possible for the moral learning and experience to be based upon, and consciously related to, a particular religion. In other schools that connection may be there for some pupils but cannot be taken for granted; and teachers and pupils in all schools live in a society in which many of the moral reference points are now less clear or less widely agreed. No school can, or should seek to, conceal from its pupils the fact that there are moral questions on which people of equal integrity and thoughtfulness may reach quite different conclusions. But moral diversity does not make moral education impossible, still less unnecessary. It is right that the curriculum should help pupils to recognise and explore differences of view both about what people accept as moral obligations and about what ultimately leads them to do so. Exploration of this kind contributes to the formation of pupils' own moral convictions. However, schools also have a clear duty to ground their pupils, by teaching and example, in those widely shared moral values like tolerance, honesty, fidelity, and

Areas of learning and experience—continued

openness to the truth which are essential for the conduct of individual and social life.

Physical

65. For practical purposes, it may be useful to identify three strands in the physical area of learning and experience. First, there are those activities which normally belong within the field of physical education and dance. They aim to develop control, coordination and mobility and to provide for the development of knowledge, understanding and attitudes. Second, there are the manipulative and motor skills which need to be applied in many areas of the curriculum and life. Third, pupils should know how the human body works, be helped to develop a healthy attitude towards it and to adopt an active way of life to keep it in good condition.

66. Young children entering school are already aware of and greatly interested in their own physical growth and skills and in those of others. Schools should provide opportunities for vigorous physical activity through adventure play and for bold movement and increasingly fine control through the use of large and small equipment. In addition, children should engage in expressive movement in response to stimuli such as music and stories.

67. The physical education programme developed out of these early activities should promote skilful body management through participation in creative, artistic activities requiring expressive movement; competition between groups or individuals involving the use of psycho-motor skills; activities leading to increased suppleness, ability, strength and stamina; and challenging experiences in various environments. The activities which traditionally provide the main contexts for physical education are gymnastics, dance, games, swimming, athletics and outdoor education. Older pupils should have access to a range of activities and it should be expected that many will have developed, by the age of 16, a high level of interest and personal performance in particular sports. Throughout the programme, factors such as continuity, frequency and intensity, in addition to breadth and variety, should be built into the work if it is to be progressive and make a real contribution to the physical and personal development of pupils.

68. Dance and other forms of expressive movement help pupils to become more sensitive and more aware of others. In school, drama, dance and movement are designed in part to explore the means of communication through movement; mime, gesture and facial expression all play their part. How far the specific skills learnt in this way translate directly into other aspects of pupils' lives will depend to a great extent upon the intensity and frequency with which they are practised and therefore how far they are assimilated into the pupil's view of himself. But, given well planned treatment in the curriculum and sensitive teaching, these skills should increase self confidence and pupils' ability to respond in appropriate ways to different people and situations.

69. Physical skills are acquired and progressively developed in most areas of the curriculum. Young children in due course need to learn to use paint brushes, pencils, and pens, and to work with increasing precision with various materials, cutting and shaping them as necessary. As pupils get older, some skills become second nature to them while new ones have to be learnt. Playing musical instruments, using hand and machine tools safely, handling scientific equipment and learning to operate a keyboard are among those activities which require careful coordination of physical and mental faculties.

70. Finally, the physical area is concerned with an understanding of how the body works and of what promotes its well-being. Pupils should learn about nutrition, dental care, hygiene, the effects of exercise and the maintenance of good health. They should understand the processes of growing up and ageing and recognise that what is 'normal' includes a great variety of physical types and attributes. These matters can be covered in topics and projects in the primary years and in home economics and biology at the secondary stage. They can also receive attention in time set aside for personal and social education and individual counselling.

Scientific

71. The scientific area of learning and experience is concerned with increasing pupils' knowledge and understanding of the natural world and the world as modified by human beings, and with developing skills and competencies associated with science as a process of enquiry. These include observing, selecting from the observations whatever is important, framing hypotheses, devising and conducting experiments,

Areas of learning and experience—*continued*

communicating in oral and symbolic forms and applying the knowledge and understanding gained to new situations.

72. Pupils need to be taught to organise the data gathered through observation and investigation conducted by themselves and others. They should look for relationships or patterns and try to explain them. They should be encouraged to seek alternative explanations, to select those which seem most probable and to test them by experiments. Thus infants who notice that plants on a sunny window need watering more often than those in other parts of the classroom may be led to an investigation both into the evaporation of water and the rate at which water is taken up by plants. Such an investigation might involve the observation of what happens to water left in saucers in various parts of the school, considerations of plants of different sizes, noting temperature differences and the effect of ventilation. With young children, fine measurement might well be inappropriate: for example, it would probably suffice to distinguish between fairly crude categories in describing temperature. In due course, children are likely themselves to discover the need to make their observations progressively more exact.

73. The emphasis should be on considering real problems. Pupils should be encouraged to handle objects, to observe phenomena, to talk about these and to take part in enquiries through which skills related to science as a process can be developed. Careful observation using all the senses, with due regard to safety, should be encouraged, so that pupils become used to looking for differences and similarities in all kinds of contexts and to seeking explanations for them. Younger children might, for example compare the feeding habits of a hamster with those of a gerbil, or objects which sink with those which float. In the second example, some children will quickly notice that some objects float higher in the water or sink more quickly than others, and they should be encouraged to follow up their observation. An ecological study or the effects of heat and water on chemical elements can be the starting points for investigations with older pupils. It is not realistic to suppose that every single opportunity can be taken to turn a question into a practical investigation, but making the most of such opportunities should lie at the heart of science teaching and learning.

74. Occasions for scientific enquiry arise in many parts of the curriculum and in pupils' experience out of school. They can spring, for example, from displays of objects on a nature table or artefacts in museums, from walks, field trips and other educational visits. In primary schools they can be found in activities such as modelling in plastic materials, where the effects of temperature on the material may be considered, and making and playing musical instruments which gives rise to questions about the various ways in which sound is produced and its pitch changed. Subjects such as home economics and CDT enable pupils to apply and investigate scientific principles, for example in the production of yoghourt or in comparing the properties of different materials. Consumer tests give opportunities for scientific investigation of products to spread into mathematical, graphical, linguistic, ethical and other fields. A topic on transport could include investigations into the factors affecting boat design, the principles of flight, the various sources of energy to provide movement, and many others.

75. Older pupils, including top juniors, should be able to devise fair tests as well as to perform experiments and to appreciate the need to repeat tests in order to ensure that the results are consistent; and if they are not consistent to be able to investigate the causes of such variation and to change the design of the experiment. Pupils of secondary age should be helped to identify variables and to design controlled experiments; they should be able to make accurate observations and precise measurements and to quantify their observations as appropriate. In the course of their investigations, pupils will need instruction and practice in the safe handling of equipment and instruments. They will need also to become acquainted with some of the major unifying themes of science such as the interdependence of living things, the properties and characteristics of materials and the relationship between structure and function. Such acquaintance should grow progressively over the years 5 to 16.

76. Scientific education involves a number of valuable processes which, although they are characteristic of the way in which the scientist works, can also be fostered in other subjects. Indeed, in the rational and logical consideration of any problem there are elements of scientific method. History and geography are only two of the subjects in which pupils should be expected to collect evidence, judge its relevance to the present purpose, identify significant features or patterns in it, offer explanations

Areas of learning and experience—continued

for them, test the explanation by reference to other evidence and arrive at a conclusion based on this process.

77. Through recording and communicating their observations and findings pupils can be helped to improve their communication skills. Scientific learning also provides opportunities to teach pupils to use books and other printed materials as sources of information and to extend their developing interests. It helps them to improve their abilities to solve problems in a systematic way, to seek solutions and to synthesise valid conclusions from their findings. It should foster attributes such as open-mindedness, flair and originality, cooperation and perseverance. It should help them to become better informed about, and competent to judge, the impact of scientific developments upon individuals and society at large.

Spiritual

78. This area of learning and experience points at its most general to feelings and convictions about the significance of human life and the world as a whole which pupils may experience within themselves and meet at second hand in their study of the works and the way of life of other people. Religious education, which has a statutory place in the curriculum, is contained within this area but is not identical with it. Sometimes it may be awe at the natural world or an aesthetic rather than an explicitly religious experience which induces this insight, or sense of disclosure. But, whatever their source and significance, such moments of insight are perhaps an indication that there is a side of human nature and experience which can be only partially explained in rational or intellectual terms. Dance, drama, music, art and literature witness to the element of mystery in human experience across the centuries and in every culture, but there are few parts of the curriculum which do not in some way show that influence. However such experiences arise it is necessary, for pupils' understanding of human aspiration and for personal growth, that they be acknowledged, reflected upon, and valued.

79. The fact that major world religions other than Christianity are now significantly represented in our society has been reflected in recent years in many Agreed Syllabuses of religious education. In these syllabuses, as in others, Christianity retains

its central place in religious education, because of its pervasive influence on this country's religious life, history and culture. However, they tend to place a greater emphasis upon man's 'religious quest' and some of its contemporary expressions in belief and practice rather than to view religious education in county and voluntary schools as a process of induction into a particular religious tradition.

80. Through religious education and other subjects as well as in school assemblies pupils can be helped to reflect upon those aspects of human life and the natural world which raise questions of ultimate meaning and purpose, and to recognise the spiritual dimension of experience. Pupils need to be introduced to some of the central elements of the Christian and other major religious traditions as they are expressed in stories, rituals, family ceremonies, communal festivals, and moral codes, and in particular to the many ways in which the Christian tradition has influenced our society. As part of their religious education, therefore, pupils will need a progressive introduction to stories of people past and present whose lives exemplify qualities universally valued; to myths which communicate religious ideas about the origin and purpose of the world; and to the way that religion makes use of symbol, allegory and analogy, and invests some of the language of everyday life (like 'light' and 'darkness') with deeper significance. Such knowledge will enable pupils during the course of their school life to appreciate the way that religious beliefs shape life and conduct; to begin to make their own response to the claims of religion; and to respect religious convictions where they cannot share them.

81. The elements mentioned above should be represented in the work throughout the age range 5 to 16 with the approach and emphasis adjusted to suit the age and experience of the pupils. For example, in the early years, though there may well be some explicit work in religious education, emphasis is likely to be placed on learning from the life and relationships of the school, discussion, stories, and religious festivals. In addition, the work with older pupils will be able to call upon their wider personal experience of life, both direct and indirect. It should also make use of their increased capacity to compare and contrast, for example, religious and scientific ways of thought and forms of expression.

Technological

82. At the heart of people's involvement with technology lies

Areas of learning and experience—continued

the constant search for ways and means to extend and enhance our powers to control events and order our environment. Technology itself enables work to be carried out more efficiently and effectively; to purchase more, better and cheaper products; and to carry out operations which human physical and mental capacities could not do unaided by the extension and refinements technology brings to those human capacities.

83. Learning about technology and its historical and social consequences, and exploring the opportunities to apply scientific principles that involvement with it makes possible, have long featured in the work of schools. Such work should continue and, if anything, be increased in scale and range. But work of that kind does not of itself make up a technological area of learning and experience sufficiently delineated and comprehensive to stand alongside the other, more firmly established, areas that should feature in a broad curriculum. The study of the impact of technology and its social and environmental 'spin-offs', however interesting, is no substitute for active involvement in the process itself.

84. All pupils throughout the 5 to 16 period should be so involved. The essence of technology lies in the process of bringing about change or exercising control over the environment. This process is a particular form of problem solving: of designing in order to effect control. It is common to all technologies including those concerned with the provision of shelter, food, clothing, methods of maintaining health or communicating with others, and also with the so-called high technologies of electronics, biotechnology and fuel extraction and the alternative technologies of the Third World. As in all learning, the involvement must be characterised by progression, internal coherence and continuity. But technology also has its content which, while not exclusive to it, is essential to the technological process. That content broadly concerns the nature and characteristics of natural and manufactured materials, and the nature, control and transformations of energy.

85. In all schools pupils need opportunities to handle materials in ways which enable them to form important concepts. Young children can be brought to understand that, while steel is hard, it is also elastic; that glass is not only brittle but strong; that some materials deform irrevocably when stretched while others regain their former shape; that some materials change

their characteristics when heated. Pupils need to learn that these characteristics are important when it comes to choosing materials for the solution of particular problems. In addition they need to be aware of aesthetic qualities such as texture, colour and form. It is not solely in workshops and laboratories that information about materials is gained, but in all parts of schools, in homes and in the general environment.

86. Equally important is the concept of energy with which all technologies are concerned. Pupils in primary schools should acquire an intuitive feel and some empirical knowledge about ways in which energy can be stored, transformed and, above all, applied to control. Torch batteries, inflated balloons, water, springs, rubber bands, plants, and falling objects and human muscle all provide starting points for exploring the harnessing and translating of energy. In the secondary school the utilisation of energy can be quantified and costed and notions of efficiency and the optimal utilisation of energy should become explicit factors in learning.

87. Even at a very early age, pupils can begin to gain confidence in their ability to get to grips with the world about them; to be active participants as well as users and spectators. For example, the familiar primary school activity of making a model of a bridge, a crane or other vehicle may sharpen the pupil's perception of the world and can lead on, through discussion, to a widening of his or her social perspective. Such modelling can be readily extended to provide some involvement and insight into the process of technology; for example, designing a model crane that will actually lift, a bridge that will support a load, or a vehicle that will perform a specified task such as covering a set distance in a set time. In undertaking this more active task, the techniques that the child may use, in the first instance, may be largely empirical; technology at this stage has sometimes been called 'making things work better'.

88. At the secondary school, the confidence to control things should be growing. There should be a qualitative change in the process of solving problems. If a crane, bridge or vehicle is designed and made, the task will be informed by a wider knowledge of the properties and limitations of materials, and, where appropriate, by some understanding of scientific principles. The activity of designing should have become systematic and should progress from problems in the immediate environment to those which are more remote such as devising ways of saving fuel in school or the automatic watering of plants during

Areas of learning and experience—*continued*

the school holidays. Designing should also include a more thorough analysis of the problem, including such essential aspects as fitness for purpose and cost in production and use. There may be a greater necessity for gaining knowledge and skills which are not already possessed, or utilising what is learned in several subjects. As in the world of industry and commerce, opportunities will occur for pupils to work in teams, each member taking on a particular role or contributing a specialist knowledge or skill. There will be a matter of planning production, of making to appropriate standards, of trying out, evaluating and possibly modifying. This total process is characteristic of CDT and the physical sciences, but the problem, solution and the process itself can emanate from biology, chemistry or from work in the humanities or social studies. The outcome need not be a piece of hardware. The devising of a new traffic flow system around a school requires no artefact, but it is none the less designing and technological in nature. Similarly, the collection, coding, storage and manipulation of data, such as pupils encounter in courses on computing or information technology, utilise the same essential features of control. Simple systems design is well within the capability of many pupils and indeed is essential to some subjects such as electronics.

89. The technological area must also include the progressive development of appropriate attitudes and in this all subjects can contribute. Technology should be depicted as neither a 'good' nor an 'evil' influence but one which gives rise to economic and social questions. There is a risk that children, and the adults from whom they learn, could adopt the view that technologies have a power of their own. They do not. It is the responsibility of schools to stress that technology is about people controlling things, not things controlling people.

Elements of learning

90. The second perspective for schools to consider (*see paragraph 25*) is that of elements of learning: the knowledge, concepts, skills and attitudes which all schools should seek to develop in their pupils. For the purposes of planning the curriculum it is useful to regard these elements as a separate checklist from that of the areas of learning and experience, even though the elements are acquired in the context of the areas and are therefore inseparable from them. The four elements, which

are developed through all nine areas, are discussed in general terms below. They will be dealt with in more detail in papers on particular subjects and aspects of the curriculum in this series.

Knowledge

91. There is so much knowledge which is potentially useful or of intrinsic interest that syllabuses are often overladen with factual content built up by unregulated accumulation or tradition. In view of this, and because knowledge itself continues to expand rapidly, schools need to be highly selective when deciding what is to be taught.

92. The criteria for selecting content should be in the aims and objectives which a school sets for itself. That which is taught should be worth knowing, comprehensible, capable of sustaining pupils' interest and useful to them at their particular stage of development and in the future. It should be chosen because it is a necessary ingredient of the areas of learning and experience or because it has an important contribution to make to the development of the concepts, skills and attitudes proposed.

93. The choice of appropriate content should be a joint enterprise of the staff as a whole, whose task it is to identify the knowledge which applies across areas and elements of the curriculum and also that which is specific to certain subjects or aspects. One benefit of this approach is that it enables the staff to know the full extent of the knowledge to be imparted and to teach it more effectively by making appropriate cross-references and avoiding unnecessary duplication and omissions. In making their selection, teachers should reject content which contributes relatively little to pupils' education or which cannot be justified on the criteria mentioned above; removal of any excess will make room for more desirable content as well as more practical applications of that which is included. In all this teachers need the support of parents, governors, advisers, examiners and employers.

94. Necessary factual information is best learnt in interesting contexts in which pupils can see its significance and importance. If it is to be committed to memory because it is frequently needed, as in the case of multiplication tables, this is best done when patterns, relationships and meaning have been perceived and understood.

Elements of learning—*continued*

95. The existence of modern facilities for the storage and retrieval of data by electronic means and the availability of the traditional sources of information such as libraries, require that pupils should be taught how to find out what they need to know for a particular purpose and how to interpret and check it.

Concepts

96. Concepts are generalisations usually arrived at through a process of abstraction from a number of discrete examples. They enable pupils to classify and to organise knowledge and experience and to predict. Some, such as refraction, are specific to certain subjects. A number of concepts – for instance temperature and energy – can be explored through work in a number of areas of the curriculum. Important concepts need to be identified, and understanding them made an important outcome of teaching and learning. Some are understood by most children by the time they start school – similarity and difference, for example – but need to be further developed; many more are learnt incidentally both in and out of school.

97. However, pupils need to understand a number of concepts which may not be encountered casually, or are not readily grasped because of their complexity. For example, the concept of change might be approached with young children through noticing the seasons of the year and the changes associated with them; through cooking, when the changes produced by baking, whipping and dissolving are examined; and through studying the locality and the children's families, examining artefacts, photographs and pictures to establish those things which have changed since the parents were children and those which have continued the same. Similar approaches are equally appropriate for older pupils but the level of understanding and analysis should be higher. The older juniors should seek explanations as to why certain changes have come about in, say, the occupations of villagers or in the length of daylight at different times of the year. In secondary schools the same themes can be approached in greater depth, perhaps by the study of the industrial revolution and the effects of migration through history and geography, or in physics and chemistry by a study of the internal combustion engine.

Skills

98. A skill is the capacity or competence to perform a task. At

a simple level skills may refer to actions or movements performed semi-automatically as a result of repeated practice, or to intellectual processes carried out by the use of facts committed to memory. On another plane skills may involve the application to different tasks of complex thought processes drawing on understanding and abilities of a high order.

99. Skills may be more or less specific: hitting a ball correctly; using a cutting knife accurately and safely; reading and writing effectively. Many are applicable in a variety of contexts and are therefore important not only in their own right but in giving pupils the confidence and satisfaction which come from achieving useful goals at appropriate levels (since there are obviously degrees of skilfulness). Many skills cluster together – the skills of communication, for example. Skills are best acquired in the course of activities that are seen as worthwhile in themselves by children and teachers alike, and in contexts which ensure that the children are able to apply them as well as to master them, in particular in the precision and control with which they use them and the judgements they apply concerning their appropriateness.

100. Skills which need to be developed in schools may be conveniently grouped as follows

Communication
the ability to listen, speak, read and write effectively
the ability to use and interpret non-verbal and graphical means of communication

Observation
to observe accurately using all the senses and a variety of instruments, such as hand lenses and measuring devices
to observe details, similarities and differences
to observe sequences

Study
to discriminate and to classify
to recognise relationships (patterns) in data
to select and extract information from a variety of sources
to weigh and interpret evidence and to draw conclusions

Problem-solving
to ask pertinent questions
to propose alternative hypotheses and to help to design ways of testing them
to carry out fair tests

Elements of learning—*continued*

to apply knowledge and concepts to the solution of real-life problems
to predict on the basis of experience and data
to make informed choices

Physical and practical
to coordinate bodily movement and finer manual skills
to develop craft skills – cutting, shaping, joining
to select appropriate tools and items of equipment and to use them effectively
to write legibly
to use keyboards

Creative and imaginative
to envisage life at other times, avoiding anachronism, and in other places; to imagine life as it may appear to other people
to express ideas
to devise and design in various media including sound and movement

Numerical
to estimate and to measure
to understand and to formulate accurately relationships expressed in the four operations of arithmetic
to use numerical and spatial relationships and elementary graphical and statistical data

Personal and social
to meet personal needs such as dressing oneself, handling a knife and fork, using a telephone
to adjust to different social contexts
to consider others' views
to contribute, cooperate and take the lead as appropriate within groups
to accept responsibility

101. Promoting these skills requires attention to the type and range of classroom activities. The successful development of oral skills, for example, requires opportunities for pupils to put questions and pursue points with the teacher; to give thoughtful, extended answers; to discuss and explore ideas among themselves in pairs or in groups both with and without the intervention of the teacher and, on occasions, to talk at some length on particular topics. In developing problem solving skills, teachers have the important task of helping pupils to

tackle problems analytically and to adopt logical procedures in solving them. At the same time pupils must be allowed to make mistakes and to follow false scents in what is essentially an exploratory process; and the teacher has to resist the temptation to give the 'right' answer, or to over-direct the pupil, otherwise the skill is not developed or practised.

102. Personal and social skills need to be practised in a variety of situations if they are to develop fully. In learning to be cooperative, for instance, pupils need experience in working in groups of different sizes and composition and with various individuals. Schools rightly provide many opportunities for social interaction in, for example, drama, team games, discussion groups, tutorials and courses of personal and social development as well as in social functions and extracurricular activities.

Attitudes

103. Attitudes may be considered as the overt expression, in a variety of situations, of values and personal qualities, to which they are closely related. Thus honesty, which is a quality of character or a value to which a person may subscribe, disposes him to display a particular attitude, for example, when he or a companion finds a purse in the street. Schools, homes and society at large are at pains to encourage values and qualities in pupils which will result in attitudes characteristic of a good citizen in a democratic, humane and free society. Some examples of such qualities are reliability, initiative, self-discipline and tolerance. They may be encouraged in the formal curriculum and the informal, and in the general life of the school.

104. General attitudes may be affected by particular situations. For example, a pupil who is generally conscientious and applies himself to his work may, nevertheless, adopt a negative approach to a certain subject because he sees little of value or interest in it or for some other reason. It is important, therefore, that schools seek to promote positive attitudes through the attention they give to content and method.

105. Imaginative play in the early years of schooling, drama, the study of history and literature, and the consideration of contemporary problems in and out of school provide opportunities for pupils to explore emotions and behaviour which they may not be able to experience at first hand and to begin to

Elements of learning—*continued*

establish their own attitudes. Entertaining visitors to the school, educational visits and community service are examples of situations in which pupils can learn to translate their own developing qualities into appropriate attitudes and behaviour. Schools, however, are only one influence upon pupils, albeit an important one. Their influence will be greater when the interest of parents is actively sought and least when they are working in direct opposition to outside influences. Particularly sensitive handling will be needed where there is potential for conflict between the values and attitudes which the school sees as desirable and the views of some parents.

Characteristics of the curriculum

106. If the opportunities for all pupils to engage in a largely comparable range of learning are to be secured, certain characteristics are desirable.

Breadth

107. The curriculum should be broad. That is to say in the terms of this paper it should bring pupils into contact with the nine areas of learning and experience and with the four elements of learning associated with them: not to involve pupils sufficiently in all these areas and elements is to leave their education lacking in some respects. As *Primary education in England*[2] demonstrated, there is an association between a broad curriculum and successful performance in aspects of language and mathematics. The various curricular areas should reinforce one another: for example (see references) the scientific area provides opportunities for pupils to learn and practise mathematical skills. Breadth is also necessary within an area and within its components: thus in the linguistic and literary area pupils should read a variety of fiction and non-fiction – myths, legends, fairy tales, animal stories, stories based on family life, adventure stories, historical fiction, science fiction, reference books, factual accounts, documents, directories and articles.

108. Class teachers in primary schools are in a strong position to arrange the interplay of the various aspects of learning since, as *Primary education in England* pointed out:

> The teacher can get to know the children and know their strengths and weaknesses; the one teacher concerned can readily adjust the daily programme to suit special circumstances; it is simpler for one teacher

than for a group of teachers to ensure that the various parts of the curriculum are coordinated and also to reinforce work done in one part of the curriculum with work done in another.

109. This does not mean that the class teacher can or should be expected to cover the whole curriculum unaided, especially with the older pupils. He or she should be able to call on the support of teachers who, as well as having responsibilities for their own classes, act as consultants in particular subjects or areas of the curriculum. This is particularly effective when such consultants help other teachers to identify objectives, to plan the teaching and learning and to evaluate it. Much is gained if they work alongside class teachers; there might well also be occasions when consultants could take full responsibility for teaching a class other than their own. Where this occurs it is important to ensure that there is close cooperation between the consultant and the class teacher so that the work done by the consultant is not isolated from the rest of the children's programme. Where consultants regularly teach classes other than their own, care is also needed to ensure that the work of the consultant's own class is not fragmented. If consultants are to teach other classes without disrupting the work of their own or to work alongside class teachers many primary schools will need some additional teaching staff and many will have to deploy their staff more effectively.

110. Primary schools generally offer a broad curriculum in the sense that all the areas of learning and experience are present to some extent. However, care is needed to ensure that breadth is not pursued at the expense of depth since this may lead to superficial work. In art and craft, for example, children may be given a wide range of work in two and three dimensions with a variety of media but may spend insufficient time on any one aspect to achieve an appreciation of the medium and to develop skills and techniques. Similarly history and geography may rightly be subsumed in some thematic or topic work but be treated very superficially.

111. Although secondary schools offer a broad range of subjects, that alone does not guarantee breadth. One reason is that each subject may be narrowly conceived, so that it presents a limited view of the subject itself and makes an insufficient contribution to the areas and elements of the curriculum set out earlier in this paper. Another reason is that for some pupils the range of subjects available may in any case be restricted by undue specialisation or to meet other special needs. Breadth and balance are even more vulnerable in years four and five if

Characteristics of the curriculum—*continued*

option systems permit whole areas of learning and experience to be neglected by individual pupils: it is important that pupils should maintain contact up to the age of 16 with all the areas and elements of the curriculum, while still exercising some choice of subjects.

Balance

112. A balanced curriculum should ensure that each area of learning and experience and each element of learning is given appropriate attention in relation to the others and to the curriculum as a whole. In practice this requires the allocation of sufficient time and resources for each area and element to be fully developed. Balance also needs to be preserved within each area and element by the avoidance, for example, of an undue emphasis on the mechanical aspects of language or mathematics, or on writing predominantly given over to note taking and summarising. There should also be a balance in the variety of teaching approaches used: didactic and pupil-initiated; practical and theoretical; individual, group and full-class teaching.

113. Balance need not be sought over a single week or even a single month since in some cases it may be profitable to concentrate in depth on certain activities; but it should be sought over a period of, say, a term or a year. Thus if work on a given topic contributes to a certain area of the curriculum or promotes certain skills, it is necessary to choose a future topic to cover other areas or skills to rectify any imbalance. Balance should also be sought in the approaches to learning. Children who are slow to master the early skills of reading, for instance, should not be confined to reading primers but should have access to a wide range of written material through reading for themselves well illustrated books at a suitably simple level or having books read to them.

114. If balance is to be maintained in secondary schools, it is essential to avoid the undue preoccupation with a relatively narrow range of content, especially in the years immediately preceding public examinations. Teaching and learning which confine themselves to examination requirements can too easily lead in a number of subjects to an overemphasis on writing of a restricted kind, reading which is confined to prescribed books, and little opportunity to address real and interesting problems. This kind of imbalance is undesirable for any pupil, but is

especially so for those of average ability who may have little opportunity for success if their strengths lie outside the limits prescribed. Examination courses should be selected by schools and designed by boards in ways that minimise these problems.

115. Within special programmes such as the Lower Attaining Pupils Programme (LAPP) or the Technical and Vocational Education Initiative (TVEI), it is equally important that pupils should retain a balanced curriculum which is enriched and not impoverished by these developments. At their best, programmes of this kind can rectify an imbalance by making the curriculum more practical and relevant to adult life for pupils and by causing schools to expand their range of approaches to teaching and learning. Specifically, pupils of both sexes and all abilities can benefit from work which enhances their understanding in the scientific and technological areas of learning and experience through subjects such as business studies, craft, design and technology, computer studies, science and mathematics.

Relevance

116. The curriculum should be relevant in the sense that it is seen by pupils to meet their present and prospective needs. Overall, what is taught and learned should be worth learning in that it improves pupils' grasp of the subject matter and enhances their enjoyment of it and their mastery of the skills required; increases their understanding of themselves and the world in which they are growing up; raises their confidence and competence in controlling events and coping with widening expectations and demands; and progressively equips them with the knowledge and skills needed in adult working life. Such a curriculum will be practical in that it serves useful purposes and is seen to do so by pupils, their parents and the wider society. Thus relevance and practicality are closely related but not always synonymous.

117. Work in schools can be practical in a number of ways. First it can be directly concerned with 'making and doing'. In primary schools children are introduced early to using paper, clay and constructional toys, to making three-dimensional shapes and to practising their skills with tools. Such activities are continued and expanded through primary and secondary schools so that most pupils will have had experience of working with a variety of materials including food and fabrics, and will have had some opportunities for designing, experimenting,

planning and testing. In addition they will have been introduced to many of the practical aspects of homemaking. All these are valuable in their own right.

118. Second, work which is not directly concerned with making and doing can often be based on practical activity. Pupils at all stages need to work and enjoy working with abstract ideas and to come to an understanding of them by drawing on their own concrete experience, observation and powers of reasoning and, whenever possible, by testing out and reinforcing their learning by reference to real examples. Some of this exemplification may be easily and regularly provided, while some may take the form of a rarer and more unusual experience: the regular application of mathematics to real situations is an example of the first; educational visits or community service are examples of the second. Often what is taught in this way has an impact which may otherwise be missed: teachers who have seen the reaction of infants to hatching chickens or of apparently blasé older pupils on first seeing or climbing a mountain will need no persuading of this.

119. Third, all that pupils learn should be practical, and therefore relevant, in ways which enable them to build on it or use it for their own purposes in everyday life. For example being read to, reading, hearing music, or taking part in a discussion, all have both a specific and a cumulative effect on the individual, especially if teachers use opportunities to relate what is being learnt to pupils' interests, to contemporary realities and general human experience. As well as becoming more knowledgeable, pupils need to become wiser and to develop an ability to draw on what they have learnt to help them live their lives more competently and with a sense of fulfilment.

120. Fourth, the more that knowledge and skills learned in school can be developed within and applied to activities that have real purpose and place in the wider world, the more clearly their relevance will be perceived by the pupils. With younger children the adoption, care and study of, say, a village pond, or a survey of the effectiveness of local public transport, call upon them to use and develop a range of knowledge and skills in pursuit of useful outcomes. With older pupils activities such as researching, designing and producing large toys for use in nursery schools and playgrounds, or bringing their intellectual

and practical skills to bear on devising solutions to real problems such as setting up a production line manufacturing boxes for plants, or designing and making a safety device to prevent pans being pulled off cookers by small children, enhance their understanding of skills, reveal the relevance of them to life and work outside the school and provide actual experience of the forces and issues that influence and impinge on problem solving in the real world.

Differentiation

121. As stated in HMI's discussion document *A view of the curriculum* (HMSO, 1980):

> The curriculum has to satisfy two seemingly contrary requirements. On the one hand it has to reflect the broad aims of education which hold good for all children, whatever their capabilities and whatever the schools they attend. On the other hand it has to allow for differences in the abilities and other characteristics of children, even of the same age . . . . If it is to be effective, the school curriculum must allow for differences.

122. Paragraphs 21 to 24 describe a variety of groupings which may be used to allow for differences in the nature of what is to be learnt, the skills to be practised, the teaching methods to be employed and the interests and abilities of the pupils. It has to be recognised, however, that simply setting up such groupings does not necessarily meet the needs of each individual member. For example, within a group formed on the basis of similar performance in a particular subject and containing, say, twenty pupils, there is still a range of competence, and work that is pitched at the level of the notional average for the group may restrict the ablest and disconcert the less able.

123. A necessary first step in making appropriate provision is the identification of the learning needs of individual pupils by sensitive observation on the part of the teacher. This may indicate a need for smaller, more homogeneous groups, regrouping for different purposes, or the formation of subgroups for particular activities. Individual work and assignments can be set to allow for different interests, capabilities and work rates so long as this does not isolate pupils or deprive them of necessary contact with other pupils or the teacher. Finally there should be differentiation in the teaching approaches; some pupils need to proceed slowly, and some need a predominantly practical approach and many concrete examples if they are to understand abstractions; some move more quickly and require more demanding work which provides greater intellectual challenge; many have a variety of needs which cannot be neatly categorised.

Progression and continuity

124. Children's development is a continuous process and schools have to provide conditions and experiences which sustain and encourage that process while recognising that it does not proceed uniformly or at an even pace. If this progression is to be maintained there is a need to build systematically on the children's existing knowledge, concepts, skills and attitudes, so as to ensure an orderly advance in their capabilities over a period of time. Teaching and learning experiences should be ordered so as to facilitate pupils' progress, with each successive element making appropriate demands and leading to better performance.

125. The main points at which progression is endangered by discontinuity are those at which pupils change schools; they also include those at which children enter school, change classes or teachers, or change their own attitudes to school or some aspect of it. Not all change is for the worse, however, and many pupils find a new enthusiasm or aptitude in new situations. Nevertheless, curricular planning within and between schools should aim to ensure continuity by making the maximum use of earlier learning.

126. Primary schools have to build on and allow for the influences to which children entering school have already been exposed and to take account of what will be expected of them in the schools to which they will transfer in due course: secondary schools must acknowledge and build on the fact that the pupils they receive have already been in school for six or more years, and that, at the age of 16, they ought to be prepared for the choices available to them at that stage. Continuity within schools may best be achieved when there are clear curricular policies which all the staff have been involved in developing and which present a clear picture of the range of expectations it is reasonable to have of individual pupils. If the goals are as clear as possible, progress towards them is more likely to be maintained. Between schools, the problem may be much more difficult, especially in an area in which secondary schools receive pupils from many contributory schools. Nevertheless, it is possible to arrive at some important, agreed objectives and often this is made easier by the existence of policies within a local education authority.

Starting school

127. Primary schools should seek to encourage and develop potential to the full, starting from the point which each child has reached on entry. This starting-point will vary considerably from child to child. Ideally, children will be using language to express their ideas and feelings, have some understanding of simple mathematical ideas and relationships, have reasonable manipulative skills and be starting to cooperate with one another. Some children will have been helped to develop such competences by attendance at nursery schools or classes. But many children will lack these competences and schools will face the difficult task of meeting such children's needs as well.

128. The majority of children enter school soon after their fourth birthday. Providing a programme that meets educational needs of a 4 year old in a class of older children presents many difficulties. The time and attention rightly demanded by the children of statutory age often mean that the 4 year olds follow a pattern of work similar to that of the other pupils, making too early a start on formal skills of literacy and numeracy at the expense of exploratory and practical activities and of the variety of language associated with them. Suitable provision is more likely to exist in LEAs where there is a policy about the admission of 4 year olds which takes account of their developmental characteristics.

The transition from primary to secondary school

129. Pupils will have already made considerable progress in their primary schools. Many will have retained their curiosity, learnt a great deal, will know how to learn and be keen to do so. All pupils will have spent a substantial amount of time on some subjects which occur in secondary timetables, notably mathematics and English. Many will be full of excitement at the prospect of entering the secondary school and working in science laboratories, workshops and other specialised accommodation, and taking up new subjects. Others may be apprehensive about their ability to cope with new demands, having had to struggle to maintain progress in their primary school. Nearly all will be entirely unused to the kinds of organisation, timetabling arrangements and the degree of specialisation common in secondary schools.

130. The secondary school needs to consider how it can make the transition from primary to secondary education as smooth as possible by trying to ensure that children's personal confidence and sense of well-being are protected, and that their

Characteristics of the curriculum—continued

learning continues with the minimum of disruption. On the whole, schools have been more successful at these transfer points in looking after the pastoral welfare of pupils than in achieving curricular continuity. Yet the two are interdependent and an important aspect of pastoral care lies in promoting success in the main business of the school, which is learning.

131. Continuity of learning may be facilitated in a number of ways. First, it is easier if both primary and secondary schools have an appreciation of what each other is aiming to achieve both in general terms and in specific areas of the curriculum. Second, effective systems of records help to remove that ignorance of previous work done which often leads to low expectations, needless repetition and misunderstanding. Folders of pupils' work can often be more revealing and useful than the cryptic summaries of some record cards. Third, secondary schools might more often try to adopt the exploratory styles of learning which are characteristic of good primary school practice. Children who have learnt to find information for themselves, to make judgements about the direction their work should take and to pursue an interesting line of enquiry as it presents itself, lose an important element of enjoyment and pleasure in their education if such opportunities are suddenly denied them. The essence of such an approach is not dependent upon having a primary school form of organisation, although some secondary schools have experimented successfully with arrangements whereby younger pupils are taught a number of subjects by one teacher. Even with a more subject oriented organisation, the work can and should consist of a number of teaching approaches and learning styles: instruction, explanation, enquiry, discussion and factual learning, for example.

Education after 16

132. There are many routes open to pupils after the age of 16. Some will leave to enter employment, which may or may not involve further education at a college. Others will continue in full time education in schools or colleges of further education where they may follow academic or vocational courses or training schemes. There are many courses at this stage and consequently there is no single curricular framework. Some courses, such as Advanced-level courses of the General Certificate of Education, are predominantly academic and point towards higher education. Others, more likely to be provided in further

education than in schools or sixth form colleges, may be more technical and vocational. Some post-16 courses provide for those who wish to improve upon their Ordinary level or Certificate of Secondary Education qualifications. There are proposals which seek to broaden the curricula of students following traditional A-level courses (AS level*) and through the Certificate of Pre-Vocational Education (CPVE) to bring within a coherent framework some of the diverse provision of non-advanced courses provided in schools and colleges for one-year students. It is important that post-16 education (and education and training) take account of students' experiences at school.

133. During the period of compulsory schooling schools have the task of providing an education which places young people in the best possible position to take advantage of existing and future opportunities. This is best achieved by a broad pre-16 education in which what is learnt is applicable and useful, and which offers pupils sound and comprehensive advice. It can no longer be assumed that education post-16 will be consecutive with compulsory schooling, and it is more than ever likely that people will return to education and training later in life. Education at school, therefore, needs to engender positive attitudes towards education itself, to recognise individual strengths and to encourage pupils' interests. This is especially important in view of diminishing employment opportunities.

Assessment

134. Assessment is inseparable from the teaching process since its prime purpose is to improve pupils' performance. It should help teachers to diagnose pupils' strengths and weaknesses; to match the work of the classroom to their capabilities; to guide them into appropriate courses and groups; to involve them in discussion and self-appraisal; and, in reports and at meetings, to inform their parents of progress. A second purpose is to enable the teachers to see how far their objectives are being met and to adjust them and their teaching approaches accordingly. This is best done by reviewing pupils' progress in the light of what the teachers have set out to do.

---

*The proposed 'advanced supplementary' courses designed to be taken alongside A-level courses and requiring about half the time.

135. If schools are to fulfil these aims of assessment, development is needed in three main areas: clearer definition of expectations as expressed through the aims and objectives of curricula and schemes of work; improved methods of assessment in the classroom on a day-to-day basis; and improved methods of recording and reporting progress.

136. Improvement in performance must be measured against a clear identification of what it is hoped pupils will experience, learn and master. This in turn requires that aims and objectives be known and expressed in schemes of work which set out the content, concepts, skills and attitudes to be acquired and the teaching approaches and learning resources to be used. It follows that pupils need to be given tasks which allow them to demonstrate their competence across the range of performance expected of them. In this sense the assessment process is an integral part of the curriculum. Not all schools have such detailed schemes of work and, where they do, assessment and recording are seldom based on the detailed expectations set out in them.

137. Assessment involves a mixture of techniques, many of them subjective, which the teacher learns with experience to apply to day-to-day observation of how pupils perform across the range of tasks, including discussion and questioning, and to the scrutiny of written work. While few teachers articulate fully the measures which they use, or the yardsticks which they apply to performance, these forms of assessment have the virtue of being an integral part of classroom activity. A range of techniques should be used to suit the purpose and the activity.

138. The Assessment of Performance Unit has conducted surveys of mathematics, English, foreign languages and science to discover how pupils of all abilities approach and perform tasks in these subjects. It has described frameworks for assessment and how to use them and has developed many new techniques of assessment, some of which are capable of adaptation for use by teachers in their schools. Work is also in hand to suggest teaching strategies which will enable pupils to avoid many common errors and misconceptions.

139. Much of the assessment described above has to go on in the busy environment of the classroom and must be largely impressionistic, though teachers need additional time to record their impressions. From time to time also, informal assessment

needs to be supported by more objective forms of testing, such as class tests and examinations devised by the teacher, which should be closely related to the work in hand. Similarly, graded assessments, which have become common in recent years, should reflect the full range of classroom activities. Care must be taken to see that tests do not dominate the work and that they do not so itemise the work that coherence is lost. Occasional use needs to be made also of standardised tests, particularly tests of reading and numeracy, to help in establishing a base line of performance, for screening purposes, or for the diagnosis of particular difficulties. While these tests have the advantage of greater objectivity, they can too easily be divorced from classroom work and their use should therefore be limited.

140. Recording and reporting progress are the more helpful if the findings can be used by others, as well as teachers and pupils, to illuminate current strength and weaknesses and show specific ways of improving performance. Often, however, characteristics of performance are merged into a series of global marks or grades which are of little use as a guide to future learning needs. Because the record is 'general' the report, designed to inform parents and others, is often similarly unhelpful. 'Could do better' provides no indication of which specific aspects of the work need improvement. Good practice does exist, however, and it is invariably related to specification by the teacher of clear learning targets and discussion of them with individual pupils. In this way pupils do not need to wait for a report to learn how they are progressing. The learning targets and progress towards achieving them are shared between teacher and pupil.

141. In view of current and prospective developments in external examinations, for example in criterion-referencing and profiling, there is a growing need for judgements about performance to refer specifically to the actual merits of that performance. Broader aspects of achievement and experience are being identified and will feature in the assessment, grading and certification of the General Certificate of Secondary Education and in records of achievement. These features should also apply to the assessment of pupils in schools.

Conclusion

142. This paper suggests an approach which is designed to ensure a coherent, broad and balanced curriculum for all pupils irrespective of the size, type and location of the schools they attend. While there will be variations from school to school according to the opportunities which the immediate environment affords, for example, and the enthusiasms and strengths of individual teachers, such differences should not lead to the sacrifice of any necessary aspect of the curriculum.

143. The other papers planned in this series* will deal with specific subjects and aspects of the curriculum. It is intended that they will be compatible with the framework suggested here and that, taken as a whole, they will enable schools to determine how topics, aspects and subjects in both the formal and informal work of the school may contribute to the areas of learning and experience and to the elements of learning which in this paper are proposed as the two main perspectives of the curriculum. As discussion documents they are starting points for professional debate, and teachers, headteachers, LEAs and others will be invited to consider each and all of them and to respond as seems appropriate.

---

*One has already appeared: *English from 5 to 16*. Curriculum Matters 1 (HMSO 1984.)

References

1 *Education 5 to 9: an illustrative survey of 80 first schools in England.* HMSO, 1982.
2 *Primary education in England.* HMSO, 1978.
3 *9 to 13 Middle schools.* HMSO, 1983.
4 *Aspects of secondary education.* HMSO, 1979.
5 *Curriculum 11–16.* DES, 1977.
6 *Curriculum 11–16. A review of progress.* HMSO, 1981.
7 *Curriculum 11–16. Towards a statement of entitlement. Curricular reappraisal in action.* HMSO, 1983.
8 *Special education needs.* HMSO, 1978.

Curriculum Matters: an HMI Series

1. English from 5 to 16
2. The curriculum from 5 to 16